OTHER ROOMS

I0149460

THE POETRY OF
SHIRLEY POWELL

GRIM REAPER BOOKS
Pittsburgh, PA

Some of the poems in this book have appeared in *Rooms* in 1984,
reprinted in 1986, and in *May Eve: A Festival of
Supernatural Poems* (1975), *Parachutes* (1975),
Alternate Lives (1990), and
Villages and Towns (1993)

Some poems in this volume first appeared in *Alphabeat Soup,
Echoes, Home Planet News, Light, Stone Soup Poetry* (Boston), *Oxalis,
Concepts, Indigo, Mysterious Barricades, Third Thing, Poets Fortnightly,
The Woodstock Times* and *Ball State University Forum.*

This is the 178th publication of
THE POET'S PRESS
2209 Murray Avenue #3 / Pittsburgh PA 15217
www.poetspress.org
ISBN 0-92258-36-1

This book is also available in Adobe Acrobat format.

Shirley Powell is one of a small circle of poets who astonished New York and other poetry centers in the 1970s and 1980s with a new romanticism that shed modernism with all its cynical baggage. Lyrical, supernatural, narrative, and deft in portrayal of characters, Powell's poems startled many with their freshness, and their sense of being narrated by a timeless voice.

She is a prairie twister of a poet. Her people and animals occupy a remembered world of small town and rural America, but they are real--they breathe, dream, bleed and die. Her ghosts and demons spring not from myth, but from your grandmother's rocking chair. This book selects from the very best of Powell's passionate, spooky, romantic, and haunting poems.

From Reviews of Earlier Books by Shirley Powell:
  "She offers original visions of country living, strange tales unadorned with sentimentality... she merges with nature like a Native American, sensually and wholly, chewing bark of sycamore, wearing necklaces of shark's eggs, drinking rain pools."
  — Dakota Lane, *The Woodstock Times*

  "A book to receive without prejudiced expectations, letting in its wildness and innocence and rediscovering your own images of trees, earth, water, 'the moon's clothed brightness' and snow..."
  — Jeanne Fitzgerald, *Oxalis*

  "Who is this superb poet? ... she is capable of an intense poignancy in reflection, and she is mightily concerned with what it means to be a human among humans and with what it means to be a creature among creatures. She hides herself behind each page...because she is capable of hiding herself... such ability is power manifest.
  — David Castleman, *Dusty Dog Reviews*

  "This is the poetry of softly padded feet...of coolly driven power, fried dough and shelter that is based in the sun... their proletarian dignity had me spinning in my stool...They cancel our obligation to 'night of the living victim' and weaving a Wordsworthian quilt they open our souls to little and familiar things. Shirley Powell deftly mists us in nature to break our bondage to the laundry list of life."
  — Bob Tramonte, *Home Planet News*

ALSO BY SHIRLEY POWELL

POETRY

Parachutes (Mouth of the Dragon Press, 1975)
Rooms (The Poet's Press, 1984, 1986)
Alternate Lives (The Poet's Press, 1990)
Villages and Towns (The Poet's Press, 1993)

FICTION

Parachutes (Mouth of the Dragon Press, 1975)
Running Wild (Avon Books, 1981)

TABLE OF CONTENTS

Legions of Bats   9
In the Beginning   10
Steel in the Fingers Writes This Line   11
The User   12
Just Before the Migration   13
Seventy Years Ago   15
Rat Hunt   17
Puma   18
Mad Woman   19
At the Bar   20
Getting Thicker   21
Gypsy   22
Earth Song   23
When Will It Happen   24
There Is a Box   25
There Is a Sphinx   26
Grammarian's Poem   27
Clock Shock   28
Alley Oop   29
Under the Lighthouse   30
The Daughter Speaks   31
Boy in a Bubble   32
Woods, Ruth Woods   34
First Magic   36
The Quarrel   37
Margot   38
Country Visit   39
About Barbara   40
Real Poet   41
Going After Cows   42
The Fish Continues   43
Owl's Hunt   45
The Worm's Turn   46
For Snow   47
A Druid's Tale   48
Speech by an Old Deity   50
Freaks   51
The Chair   52
From Andromeda   55
Letter from the Front   56
Song 31   57
Explanations   58
Andy   60
Song 32   61
As If the Dead Need Help Too   62
Signs and Wonders   63

City Voices   64
Bird Life   65
Another True Confession   66
Grassy Covenant   67
Walking Toward You   68
Doyle Point   69
In Woods   71
And After That   72
Ghost Leg   73
Ice Ages   74
Midnight   75
Twister   76
March Flood   77
Epiphany   78
Minnewaska, Burning   79
Fever Trees   80
Communion   81
Low Clouds   82
The Search   83
Can Collector   85
The American Goat Woman   87
Under the Bed   89
Canopies   90
Dad's Ghost   91
Imago   92
The Back Bedroom   94
Lived in a Tree   96
Sea Song   97
They Can Not See Me   98
From "The Margaret Poems"   100
Year 96   107
Friends   108
Refinements   109
Before I Wrote   110

ABOUT THE POET   111

OTHER
ROOMS

LEGIONS OF BATS

Legions of bats
    stiff draperies of wings
        hung on the walls
        their shadows behind them
    under them
        stone corridors
        in the grip of the river
        a fortress of night,
        around couches of air
        damp with mammalian sleep
then the host
        the fluttering army
        spreading worn crusted wings
into sky
    netting the moon
        in webbed fingers
        their branches
crying their cryless cries
        echoing over the cliffs
        and the canyons
into pastures, and plummeting   like
            splashes of night
        falling on drowsing cattle
        cutting, lapping
                from necks of the beasts
        dumb under moon
        trickles of blood
            dark on their wrink-
            ling hides
the winged ones rising
        doing slow dances in air
        sending their silent trills
        over stone still river
flying away from the moon
        to their stations
        their shadows
keeping their hours, their days
        blood bubbles cleansing
        their hard little teeth.

IN THE BEGINNING

First lullaby?
Hunter crying for meat?
Widow's lament?
What was the first poem, where?

Can't find it in
artifacts mastodon bones
spread out on a dry creek bed

But I know it
in throat and fingers
hear it when the leaves fall
down to sleep

I write that
first poem to you over and over
as it comes to me

Time doesn't vanish

Once and once more
we raise our animal heads
stand on two legs
rename the stars

STEEL IN THE FINGERS WRITES THIS LINE

Steel in the fingers writes this line.
What can be done, must be done
with steel.

Somewhere someone is pressing a bell
but is it   where another
waits for the sound?

The line is written,
flung across these spaces.

The buzzer urges,
sightless...
at a twisted gate

THE USER

Fog arms reach
and fall away
while the steady car
tracks the road.

Farmhouses waver back long lanes
country bridges
catch at me hurrying
animals   dash at my wheels

Those others beyond the clouded windows
rush by me unhappily;
I am too transitory
to be real.

I know there is no destination
I know I am the traveler

JUST BEFORE THE MIGRATION

Something hard killed your feet
Your thin unfeathered legs splayed
from the solid rest of you
propped on your fanned and banded tail.

Alert you watched us
twitching our nervous towels

You couldn't uncurl your
blade-tipped toes
couldn't stand
                but
your beak was ready as your stern
questionless eyes

You fluttered still-strong wings
when we brought a box
that could hold you

No cats came.

Your thud at the window had brought
us   but no other
predators

Then one foot straightened
                            as if
you'd been dissembling
    the other tingled alive

You shifted the sharp shins
of your name
golden and firm under you.

A finch at our feeder
didn't distract

Your mottled breast bunched   you
lifted   taking your weapons
intact
No mercy in your coming or
your going

Mercy belongs to the nest
and you know
the nest is far away

SEVENTY YEARS AGO

Seventy years ago my grandmother
        rode a spring wind to church
        and was married
    looking around the still room
    to see   if the man she loved
        was a witness.

ample black hair puffed on her head
        eyes lively
        mouth just missing a pout
        gown to the chin
            to   the wrists
                to the floor
        delicate fingers on the young farmer's arm ...

Her lover stayed away,
    was shot in a barroom brawl the next
                            year.
She went to Montana and lived in a tarpaper shack
        snakes crawled under it
        wolves visited
        children were born and no
                            doctor
    women met in tunnels of snow
            to exchange remedies
    and when spring came
        she sometimes took the horse
            after cattle
        riding away and away
        while her young ones watched
            from the door.

She has lived to be old
        buried her husband
        two grandchildren,
        seen her children grow lean
            and grayheaded . . .

she sleeps in the long afternoons
dreaming of prairies
of wildcats that lived in the coulees,
of a lover
            who didn't come back—
she stands at a window
watching a country road.

He is walking toward her
        tall and bareheaded
        whistling and laughing
        ready at last
        to turn her life
            another way

RAT HUNT

From the roof
    where sky hangs black
    over gray gold city
the man moves down
    hearing his heels hollow on stairs
    as he passes windows blank as walls.

The cat
   crouches underneath
   black
   gray gold eyes in the dark
the cat
   sees dawn on the roof
   sleeps noon on the landing
   hunts night   below the house

arched on splintered step
claws caught in the wood
waiting for rats
          hard squeals   warm fur
          red blood in corners.

The cat
   feeds in a pool of black
   as the man's heels ring hollow
   all the way
      down the stairs.

PUMA

(After Walter Van Tilberg Clark's Track of the Cat)

Began uneasy night
     the lips of the dogs quivered in song under trees
     where the great cat had wandered.
Snow hung on the horses' hooves and their breathings
         piled in layers
         on air.
We hunted the cat
     with wind on the lake, crying its name
     to the dark for the dark's reply

Dogs and horses and men
     staggering and slipping
     into a cold ravine   saw
     the silhouette   heard
     the feline's snarl   felt
     its muscles gather   smelled
     the blood flash
when the brood mare fell, rolling and wild
     cat clamped to her neck
     claws clutching her ribs
     then leaping away

dogs thick on the hill, men cursing and turning
        their jumping mounts
shouts that the sky swallowed up
       cat   was   gone
       air   was   empty
then they shot the mare.

Drink from the cold flask, men
     into the saddles and home
the cat walks its way in the forest

dogs rest for another day, horses browse in the fields,
men fall into their beds
     while
         the wild thing follows
         wind and snow

MAD WOMAN

I, Mabel, hear the years buzz
    Someone said what happened to Mabel
    whose mother burned houses
    and someone answered they took her away
    one afternoon. She said her room was fur
    and would kill her with its great wings

I hear the years buzz
    In the hall there were owls
    and cranes with necks like esses
    webbed feet of frogs   that were men
    that suddenly were men
    I locked my door
    there were rabbits   many   weaving
        long circles
        round my room
    I ran to the window
    nuns walked near the convent
    I called and called
    after awhile men who were tall
    broke open the door
    that the dark green snails
    had sealed firm

    I was carried   bandaged in blankets
    unable to do more than wink
    down a long stair
    heads sat on the banisters
        watching

Now, I sit in a chair
    painting white pictures
    nobody sees them but me
    safer so
I have gilded my arms with a pigeon's blood
and my captors are animal lovers

Sometimes I think of the nuns
    they never come here

AT THE BAR

It was one of those nights
    when I was standing at the bar
    I saw a man bring his   hallucination   in

It sat beside him (next to me)

He didn't buy it a drink
    but patted it from time to time
    when it seemed restless
Just one more drink and we'll go home
                      he said

    A shadow seemed to grow there
    I saw a tear fall on the bar
Wait here, he told it and went back
            to the men's room

I   watched it   for him
After awhile   I   touched its hand
And that was the beginning
                  the edge
      of all the rooms
    that I keep going through.

GETTING THICKER

I think the walls are getting thicker
    I don't hear people making love of mornings any more

I thought if the telephone rang more often
    the electromagnet might revitalize the air in here

Maybe I'll begin drinking and then I won't remember
    there were thinner walls once   even windows

I dream of doors   but have forgotten how they look
    I almost (in my dream) remember
        I wake up almost remembering

Today I will walk through a wall
        breathing may not be possible
           I practice
                not breathing
It seems to me the walls are breathing now
    I am lost in the walls   like a rat scratching
        Maybe you will hear me after midnight
        maybe you will make a window
           or a door

GYPSY

You know everything.
   I turn and find the room
      is full of smoke

At night in a forest
         owls sit on your shoulders

You draw crimson wings
     on windows
I am under your bed like a nail in a box.

You trace a spider's web against the blaze
   When the fire is over
      you
will pass through   like a finger
    of smoke

      I
will stay under your bed   in a box.

EARTH SONG

Sun sings to earth in a silvering
                the turn of a wing
                in a sunpoint
brings wholeness   brings music   a clearing
that moves as I move
          that grows in the rocks
      the rocks never die

in them are the bones
               the deep places
            of evening

I have gone by and gone by
              on this road
      till the going is in me
      the wander of water on rocks
    the rocks never die

Sun sings to earth
      the turn of a wing

I have gone by
      I am the sinew of shadow
      that heralds deep places
            in evening
I have gone by.
      the rocks never die

WHEN WILL IT HAPPEN

Dog's body at the side of the road
man with twisted legs lying in a ditch
truck carrying thunder down the hill
floating, faces cold in water, those two girls

But those were dreams

Inside my ribs or somewhere
locked in my blood grains
the killer feeds and grows

he'll have me sometime, that vengeful one
it may be night   I'll be an animal
dazed by rushing lights

These are not the thoughts I want to think
I didn't ask you to come here looking:
since you did I'll tell you this, that
we will all cry murder sometime.

THERE IS A BOX

There is a box of salt
                    with a girl on it
    she has an umbrella
                        and a box of salt
                        under her arm
                    with a girl on it
    she has an umbrella
                        and a box of salt
                        under her arm
                    with a girl on it
    she

and poems are like that
        they keep being themselves
            forever
        they keep wrapping
                and unwrapping
        and there are poems
            inside them
        that look like them
    until the last shred of skin
        is peeled away

by that time the poet
        should be dead
    but even then
    she will give
            one   more   twitch

THERE IS A SPHINX

There is a sphinx sitting on my desk
   paws folded   lemon eyes filtering light
the sphinx has not smiled or spoken
sometimes in the night it will
sing without moving its mouth

It is telling me something
inside the hard rind of my dreams

Its stone will grow fur here
When its sides begin wrinkling
   in and then out
I will catch its breaths
   in quartzite
build it a moon pool
under my bed where
it can study its face

GRAMMARIAN'S POEM

Buckminster Fuller said,
" I seem to be a verb."

That made me think.
My granddad was a genuine article,
my cousin Jill an adjective
modifying every
person, place or thing.
Some men I've known are
mostly ejaculations.

The Jones we keep up with
must be prepositions:
They have so many objects.

And politicians?
They'd be pronouns,
saying they stand for
something of substance
till after the election.

As for me, I'd like to be
a conjunction,
joining all the lost parts
until my life's sentence
has more meaning.

CLOCK SHOCK

and they said that on top of
      this building uptown
   there was a clock
      they said
it never rang the hours
     but they kept it there
sometimes the hands would fly around
  the face
sometimes the face would spin around
  the hands
    and
  when the moon was in eclipse
  something would happen
    underneath the clock
at least
   some angel hair would fall
or a poem would be born

ALLEY OOP

My pup and I were in the big kitchen
    with a wood stove
    Grandma's kitchen

I climbed on her stool
    to open a cabinet door
    where she kept
        banana candy
        marshmallows
        spearmint gum

Reaching I leaned too much
    stool wavered underneath
        fell
I slid off
    onto a black and white floor

My knee was bleeding
Mama came running from the living room
Grandma followed
    "Oh, what's she done now?"

They lifted me
    righted the stool
Alley Oop my little dog
    black and white like the floor
    lay where the stool had fallen
    not moving

UNDER THE LIGHTHOUSE

(for my grandmother)

there were certain dreams you told me
             a litany
I on my cot beneath the lighthouse picture
             in its oval frame
you massaging my thin leg
             then bracing it against a pillow

You told me of girls with handsome legs
             figure skating
             tales of athletes
                being crowned
             whipped cream wishes
             perfections like a mountain
             of strawberries
                or an island
                of iced melons

                You fed me
             favorite dreams
             your fingers probing my dead
                muscles

That's why the painting of the lighthouse
             shining in the moon
             still makes me sleepy
          makes me smile
                gives me
          vague and lovely dreams

THE DAUGHTER SPEAKS

I begin to say
it is the noon sun that I have to
meet
questions you've never asked
are falling to the floor
evaporating
light in the room wavers

When you lay down that autumn
did you think of rivers shining?
Coupling on the new sheets
did you prophesy?

The mirrors glisten.
I begin to say I have to
go now
like a severed arm I
move off toward the East.

BOY IN A BUBBLE

1

I know a boy who lives in a bubble.
It keeps him alive
   he smiles at me
   I wave to him every day

My parents say he can't come out yet.
I wave to him through a window

I think his bubble grows smaller
   at night   stays on the ceiling over my bed
      in the morning it's gone.
I wish I could visit him in there.

2

I am a woman   whose son   lives in a bubble.
   he plays bouncing and running   inside it
      sleeps on a plastic floor

I am a woman   whose touch   will kill her son

3

I am a boy who lives in a bubble.
I have always been here.

Air outside is different
   there are birds in it
I can get out if I want to
      or
I can wait till the others let me.
Then no one will look at me
   but it will not be safe

The others think if they ask me to come out
I will come out.
They think if they tell me to stay in
I will stay in.

This is what they think. They have plans
They decide   When
I laugh   I laugh at them

I am getting stronger   taller   preparing
    for a certain day like the day
        that came once
        when I wasn't ready
Black birds flew by the window   crying for me
                on the right day
            my magic bubble knows
            it will have to   break

WOODS, RUTH WOODS

Every day Rafe left Ruth
in the woods that was his name
Woods and he called her by it
Ruth Ruth Woods

In the wind they moaned those
frigging pine trees and
oaks scraped each other

A house down the lane had
children in it
little white girls came
to call   Ruth made them cookies
taught them songs

brushed that long blonde hair
no wonder Indians lifted scalps
that hair was nice

Rafe wouldn't take her into town he
left her there till
after dark and hoot owls
made her light up
all the rooms

He was making money hauling trash
Get me a new truck he would say
Look how we live here
Ruth complained it ain't no life

What's wrong with it, Ruth, Ruth Woods?
You lucky you got a man
She'd shut up
before Rafe got ugly

Kept her house pure clean
so they couldn't talk about
no shiftless darkies

and then the peddler came
sold her a knife she didn't want
then told her she could
keep it for nothing and
taught her some new tunes
a dance step too

bought her a gold ring
she had to hide
kept coming back and saying
she should
meet him in town

When Rafe found out
he took the knife to her
and she ran out into
the so black woods

Ruth! Ruth Woods! he
called to her but
she was gone

Come Saturday the neighbors
went a-hunting for her among
the pines and oaks
the sleepy owls

But she was gone
for good like
somebody scooped her up
and took her down to Tupelo

The white girls missed those cookies
and those songs
At night they thought
they heard the pine trees singing
Ruth   Ruth Woods

FIRST MAGIC

Long room full of six year olds
I am teacher with a little edge of mercy left
You are student
    blank and listening
    leaning elbows on
    an old desk

      I
catch a corner of your nine o'clock dream
    you
think of spaces around words on paper

You will remember dull walls
    Catholic saints
    homilies
    your old desk
    scarred and bearing your thumb prints

Leaning over the new words you have written
    you
stare at me   In one fist you carry them
smudged   running together   to me
"Teacher, what do they say?"

Do you know better than I
that we are all mysteries?
Out of us
    come stars which line the cool East
    with firefaced Messiahs
Out of us
    comes abracadabra
Out of us and our old desks
    comes the beginning of sorrows
        the beginning twists
          in our memories
        plays back
    the anthems of Mars

THE QUARREL

When you rang the doorbell
    none of the closets would open.

Did you notice the chair
    folded into a corner
    when you came in?

The wastebasket flattened
    along the rug
      the fireplace shrank
    the window fan churned glass
      wiping stripes of moonlight
  on the walls

The room was stiff for storm
    sliding in and out of our breaths
    scratching when we spoke

MARGOT

Margot   in her last years   wore
    quiet makeup
    black slippers
    long skirts   and
    long sleeves over thin arms.

She had two gods she named Love and Art

Her aura was mystery   edited often,
    quick-quilted fictions to
    decorate all her hours.

One day a shadow fractured
    her word dazzle

She leaves us in silence, her eyes
    finally hard and terrible.
She lies on a strange bed,
    grown away from her body
that aged in spite of   all her will.

Her new lover woos her now from a
    distant place:
    a god who will lie with her
    always

COUNTRY VISIT

for Emilie Glen

You saw a snowy owl
that was really an arm
of a white birch tree.

You saw fire-eyed phantom deer
in smeared dark
beyond car windows;

you saw chimney smoke as a woman
sifting your hair in
her aromatic fingers.

You ran from our thick spring mud
that sucked at everything,
insatiable baby.

Fallen trees made a bruise
on some dream you were having—
you screamed your way from rock to rock
and nourished your feet at a waterfall.

You felt the close bald stars
making fear shadows
which our moon pulls by ...

You went home
and wrote a poem.

ABOUT BARBARA

No copy I,
as she once thought;
nor copy she, it's true.

She was like me,
and I, like her;
but we were different, too.

She stared the moon
full in its face
and never could withdraw,

while I,
more tender of my needs,
lived ravenous and raw.

We both saw monsters
clearly, fondling them
like snakes.

She, bitten first, subsided
while I invent
escapes

REAL POET

On the death of Barbara Holland

My eyes hurt.
I think of hers,
so blurred she learned
to speak the lines
without seeing them

She burned all messages,
leaving only the poems
alive.

Even she, the marvel-maker,
drifts now
and her words go out,
sparkles beyond my fingers
to touch, my mouth
to try.

GOING AFTER COWS

Granddad led the way
to gray boulder
(duck landing) to cross the branch
and then uphill

The bellwether
came even before
he slipped the halter
on her neck

She followed
down through daisies
and wild carrot
to pig sties and
to barns

Animals always did
what Granddad wanted.

Even the sick hen lay still
while he reached inside her
with a spoon to take her egg
"I thought it mighta
broke in there," he told me.

He cut off the heads of cockerels
every week at an old tree stump
He'd turn them free to flop
The other chickens watched but
didn't run away

When he went after cows
the cows came as if
he had holy wafers
in his dusty pockets

as if he knew the real
names of those cows
their long-ago desires

THE FISH CONTINUES

The fish has died before this

if it is a fish

it moves though water

as a thought

given flesh

might swim

Each panel it makes

and pushes aside

to get to the place

it is going again

The fish has lived before this

if it is a fish   it is not

puzzled

at the sameness

of its dream

it hunts out the identical water

the exact molecules

that caressed its length

before this

after this

The fish continues

if it is a fish

OWL'S HUNT

Owl in halflight
    trailing cobwebs of old stars
    over meadows
blood of small things
        whirs
in your long feathered ears

In the first stops of light
    sounds sink to earth
    and are frozen
    as your wings seem in mid-flight

White roads wrench underneath you
lean trees rise
    and the mercy of daylight
    draws back
      as you fly
      as you call

THE WORM'S TURN

All around us is a sound continuous like rain

    but not rain.
Bits of leaves lace the ground
thick caterpillars fall and crawl and eat

We have killed them all day.
Juices of green growing things spurt
    from them their black coverings erupt they
    die
    on our fingers
    under foot

Their twins remount the buildings
climb trees
drop from roofs
munch every leaf.
        They come   we kill   they come

There is a sound everywhere around us
  a sound of soft devouring
            steady uncontrollable
      like rain

FOR SNOW

I lived in snow, a snow house
while the white sky peeled
and slipped down
gathered by trees and the glad ground.

and I lived in snow
wore it for hats   heaped it over the hours
ate it as it turned to nothing
under my tongue

It was no misfortune   living in snow
sodden and chill
watching it fall and grow
fall and grow

I chewed bark of an old sycamore
tough leftover fern
dried blueberries
hard on their canes
from the summer
the few hickory nuts squirrels missed

Living in snow sledding
the hills   building ethereal castles
I animated snowwoman
carrying my dead white burden
everywhere

Of course I was frozen alive
to be found in somebody's April
lying in a flooded field crying
for snow.

A DRUID'S TALE

I will tell you
    your next dream

There is a hemlock with a gaping thick lipped
      mouth in its side
You walk down a long hill
        in the country
fallen leaves hide spiders
        doodle bugs
          snakes
spring peepers
   bounce their voices
      through the wet woods

You watch this tree
      trading places among
      other trees
sometimes it dozes on the hillside
      mouth agape for breathing
other times you've found it
      by a stream
    screaming a frozen warning
      you think you can almost hear

The other day you sit home
   at your dining room table
   pausing between spoonfuls
   of yogurt

The tree with its staring wound
   rattled your window
   you jump and fling down
     the blind.

It's this tree or you
            odds favor the tree
        which refuses to honor
        the ancient customs of trees
    while you are a traditional person who
        thinks that when in the country
            you must walk in the woods.

Now there are many trees, mostly the beeches
    that tremble as you pass
            under their burgeoning leaves
                spirit holes widen
    their voices come to you as you move
down the hill
        you had thought
        the spring peepers
    were making this clatter
    but it is really the forest itself

Someday soon you'll decipher the language
    they quaver, the hickories, the maples
            for it is easy
                the maimed sentinel tree
    tries to show you
"You are one of us," is the message.
        "Come join us."
    Sap congeals on your skin,
    bark grows
            a dainty oak leaf
            lifts itself out of your finger
What if you don't wake up?

SPEECH BY AN OLD DEITY

I am the trees,
   and the trees are breaking.
Cold fog presses my eyes
   with its negligent thumbs ...
I am your enemy
   weakening walls which
    the currents
     caress.
Why do you call to me over and over,
   standing a long time in the road,
  creek water tasting your lavender
feet?
The maelstrom is silent.
Every cloud falls without sound—
All around you branches are broken
   and floating—

I am the trees: the hickories, oaks, the pines,
   and the water-soaked birches.
I have always been
   only the trees
    and the trees are
     breaking.

FREAKS

Freaks with their crazyquilt faces
　　lumped backs　　mismatched arms and legs
freaks have their eyes on you

Freaks remember.
They follow you through doorways
sidling under your arms
they are thinking an old conversation
that doesn't begin or end
they show their stumps　　roll their tongues
　　　but do not speak

You will have to guess their screams
　　　pick the pits of their thoughts
　　　　　out of your breakfast

On a fast elevator　　they are leaning
　　　toward you
　　trying as always to capture
　　your stare
　　　they smile; perhaps they will
entertain
　　they preen and fawn at your knees
　　into the wells of their eyes your face
　　disappears
They are strengthened　　You jerk to an exit
　　　drag a club foot

THE CHAIR

It was a rocker
      old and armless
     sitting by an upstairs window
     where the seven sisters slept ...
It belonged to the grandmother
      it came with her from Ireland
     when she was sixteen
It rocked with its own squeak
    a sort of cracking sigh
  and no one used it but the grandmother
      who sometimes sat there
    piecing quilts ...

The girls who slept in that room
      often woke at night
   to the familiar squeaking sound
   and watched the rocker
   rocking slowly
     and then faster
     and then faster
    no one sitting in it
They'd cover up their heads and try to sleep
The smallest girl   occasionally would sleepwalk
  she rode the rocker on those nights
  faster faster fast asleep
Her sisters woke her gently as they could
    and she would scream with fright
  at waking in the rocker
        that could rock
alone

One night when there was moonlight all around
    the sisters heard a rattling at
      the window
  they shivered though the air was warm
    the rocker
    began rocking
      wider and wider
    fasterfaster
   turning and turning

It fell on one side and almost like a live thing
             came to rest. One of the
                 rungs had broken
    The grandmother died that night
             full of years
             and almost blind
The sisters were so frightened of the chair
       their father tore the rocker
          into parts and burned it all for firewood
          in the wintertime
And as the last of it was burning black
          the door to the upstairs began
       to open and to close
             there was a coldness
          on the stairs that seldom went away
They lay at night and dreamed the rocker had
returned
          they thought they heard it rocking
    the youngest girl would sleepwalk nights
          and ride the invisible rocker
             until she fell exhausted
             to the floor
Her sisters were too terrified to wake her

One morning when they lifted her
       they found her dead
  and after that the rocking stopped
          except for stormy nights
       when there were tiny screams
       within the walls   and the squeak
          of a rocking chair

The house is gone now
          three old women still live on
       the others dead   are sleeping in the woods
    around the house or where the house had been
Their faces all are blurred
    their voices are forgotten ...

The living and the dead
      slip in and out of dreams
   and there are times when worlds
      so intertwined bleed into
         one another
      a chill lies on the spine
   the eyes jerk upward
         like foxes gone to earth
   the things that were
         have disappeared
      into the things that are.

FROM ANDROMEDA

Rings of holy fire ...
   a country made of flame
     spread over the earth
  exotic birds with jungle in their yellow eyes
     melted in the heat
    thunder came out of the mountains
      on great wings
    and copulated with the women
   there were giants on the earth
    from them conceived
  that tore down cities
   and sank them
   like the ships that char
    the bottom of the sea—

And rings of holy fire
   have blinded all the people
    they were a claw of conquest
   and they prospered
  find them now
    their cities are destroyed
   their children have no quickness
   to break open wombs
  they have gone down
   and roaches crawl among
    their bones ...

Rings of holy fire
   encircle earth
     that   from Andromeda
   look lovely in the night

LETTER FROM THE FRONT

I saw a hawk yesterday, white
    underneath as it flew, showing its
    banded tail.

Its complaining cry shrilled down as
    it sailed the air over white pines.

Later that day, the same bird passed;
    a shadow between us earthlings and
       the sun.

Silent this time, it kept its thoughts
       close.

Like me, the hawk eats, needs to settle down,
    feed dependents. Like me, it screams
    dissatisfactions or some days
    takes currents as they lift or
    lower
       Yet that hawk is wild, its
       dreams are blood.
          Its muscles
    swell against the furred and feathered
       every day

That winged fury
       might hurl a bomb
       if it could
       might die surprised
    vaporized inside its own rage

Beneath my shoulder blades
       a hawk beats to
       fly free
    to let go
       lightning,
    to attack, long taloned,
  dive down to viscera,
       destroy!

SONG 31

Who has remembered my name?
   Out of the hours of drinking of
      falling in bed with this one
         with that one
who has remembered my name?

When the soft sky yields
   to the bruising of night
      flames and then darkens
I have seen birds rise on invisible air
   before falling into the night   into sleep
If I could I'd call the names of those birds
   I'd wind my words into their wings

I am the sleeve   that the dark places fill

I have seen women rising out of their sleep
   with long hair   their faces the color of love
I have watched handsome men swimming in streams
   seen water gather on their arms and
      the down on their legs
I have seen children   the brightness of mornings
   touched forests and felt the moth's wing
      warm under my arm
I have lain by the ocean   have known it could kill me

Who remembers my name?

The people are birthing   are dying
   moving inside and outside me
I am the skip in your heatbeat
   the threat that you feel before dawn

   alone in the angle of death
      in the swiftness of life
      in that touch of bright water

No one
   remembers my name
      for it is   lightning that never was seen
        it is   the ringing of bells
           on an island at night

EXPLANATIONS

Somebody tried to kill me.
It was on East Broadway and he had a chunk
of sidewalk raised in his hand
to thunder on my head.

My back was turned. I
never saw him really except
that he was tall
didn't know him

Two men also behind
wrestled away the chunk of concrete and
he ran

We tried to catch him but
he disappeared among the crowds of people or
inside some anonymous building

Did he wait awhile pick
another victim and brain her
with a heaviness of metal or of stone?
And did she sag this time
towards sidewalk with hardly room
between the walkers and her form to
heap itself down there and bleed ?
Did he run away again or stay
to savor what he'd done?

Other questions:
Was I his first intended murder
or were there chosen others
heads broken for no reason
they would ever know?

It would be fine to think
he tried just once
and that time failing
looked for help to mend
his own broken head
never doing violence before or since

I haven't seen him in my dreams
or elsewhere unless
I could have   without recognition

Without recognition death walks behind
and if he misses runs away

Why did I chase him that time?
What do we want from death?
We probably wouldn't like
his explanations

ANDY

The main thing was the baths

Ordinary life merely occurred
oatmeal
storefronts
tv bilge

      But   at night
and into some lost days
he ruled at the baths
on 1st Ave. near Houston
or other places
              had invitations
by halflight
           everyone in love
or almost with his eyes
changing green   changing blue
                          while
his red mane arched stallion-like
over the strong neck

His eyes destroyed
and were destroyed
     holes in a raped face now.
Adonis blinded.

SONG 32

      could the words cut
clean and the foul gush fall
      could the face become
clear
      the voice be known as dawn is
      and as expected

      could I step
            out of the dark
               close
             as your breath
             and the peace between
               breathings

could you take hold
         of my hand
        read my words
          in your fingers my words
        by your own throat's clutch

could something I say
catch you at midnight   lean down
    from your ceiling
      curve into your head and lodge there
            shuttered in sleep
            invisible
            thriving

I would be caught   in your cells
                          an
            infinitesimal genie
                        quick
          as your blood forever

AS IF THE DEAD NEED HELP TOO

I was in a rowboat near shore
just sitting there staring at
the water silvery and clear showing me

a woman's hand and then her arm
I reached and pulled into the boat
a woman warmly dressed in red and
other colors. Stiff and pale she
wasn't even wet. She lay there in the bottom
of the boat while I wondered
what to do with this body

And then she said "I'd like to be
put back where I was." I know the dead
don't speak and still she did. I lay her back where
it was cold   She settled softly down.

I left and confused told a man I knew
I'd found a body. He came back with me and
I hoped she'd talk to him
not wanting this odd talent of
hearing what others cannot

A few nights later I
was carrying a dead man's body
everywhere I went   hoping no one
would realize his state I sort of
propped him up as I was
walking   and he talked to me
just mundane things but still ...

Even after waking
I've decided to avoid
the dead. You'd think
they wouldn't call attention
to themselves unless it was important.

SIGNS AND WONDERS

Once I saw
    huge trucks rising out of night fog
        roaring they floated beyond me
        leaving me lost in a new time

I saw in summer at low tide
    a collie's pelt in the ocean
        shredding   to stiff needle hairs
           at beach edge

In a small western stream   a fish
    swam to my feet
    leaped out of the water
    twitched once and died staring at me

Let me live long enough to discover
    the end of the island in daylight
        every inch of me etched with
           wonders and signs
        myself a sea relic
           an answer
        drenched   indelible real

CITY VOICES

That was the night
the first saw whet owl called
herringbone body and blond
eyeballs at the window

I was three flights down before
she threw her rope of wings
into the tall plane tree's
shadow

The owl snapped her beak
Branches took me made me
bleed then enfolded
me in my pajamas

That night she killed four mice
on an island at 95th
& Broadway
mice born there
worrying the sand
waiting for traffic to leave
She swooped four times and
they died fast

Other owls come now
the great horned and
the gray

I follow and learn all
except flight

Halloween I spent at Potter's Field
with a barred owl and   a screech

I'm ready for anything

So far no feathers   but
I can feel hoots in my chest
teaching my throat

BIRD LIFE

To us it's mainly wings and
effortless flying
soaring and turning in patterns
even ubiquitous pigeons
synchronize in Manhattan's
stagnant   air

To you it is lightness and
being one tenuous muscle
occasionally able
to rest on the invisible.

It is getting and giving
eating and being eaten

dying and living
all of it quick and bright colored
    painful or
        delectable

and it is poetry   singing

a mesh of radiance
rising and falling

finer and truer than

we are

raven and wren
swallow and sparrow

whispers of lightness
moments so whole
we cannot know them we
cannot guess

ANOTHER TRUE CONFESSION

Accuse me of a crime.
   I'm a murderer in thoughts
   that have canceled populations
     rivaling Chicago's
                Call me
   lascivious, a wanton
     glutton, heretic,
  welsher on old debts, liar,
    thief—a
         deviate,
  malcontent, hypocrite,
    what you will.

I am all.
   I have been a politician,
   weaver of words, lover of
   waterfalls; any base thing.

I'll trade poems for mangled promises, tell
   a story to make up for harsh words
                If
  the wind is right, you will be
  satisfied and
             occasional satisfaction is
  as much as our little lives allow

GRASSY COVENANT

It's Sunday and the grass
is calling. It calls at a certain stage
of dryness, later in the day,
and when it's tall, all clover-filled like now

The grass desires cutting, being brought
to heel. Otherwise, it's too full of itself
and centipedes and bumble bees.
Mice and voles and striped snakes like it tall and
dense

Grass these days is smart;
it knows too much success is enervating
and is populated with unwanted company.

It calls me to lend a hand, to
trim it back, to discourage ticks and
spiders, the endless ants, the irksome
beetles God loves so

I plug in my weed whacker, gas up
my power mower, get ready to
perform my righteous deeds

Snakes wiggle away to bushy spots
Voles and comrades choose another yard
or go underground, the ants lie low
as I roar over the slopes and straight passages
over the clovers, white and red
They lose their pretty heads
and grasses pass into the gathering bag

I'm never done of course

The grass calls often
now that I've learned its language, now
that I know its subtle needs, its
longing for being brought low,

No permanent damage

WALKING TOWARD YOU

I am walking toward you.
    Like the alphabet you
        cannot be avoided.
It is night and the sky has no memory;
    you are another shadow that does not speak.

I have come out of sunbursts into forests.
I am snapping at air   scattering trees—
    there may be a dragon farther on
        or wolves
    that leap from behind/
Like the stars that seem to happen but
    only continue,
you wait.

My steps hold the rim of the world;
without me you have no quickness,
    and only the songs
I have not written/

I will not be enough for you,
    still you must have me.
Perhaps you are nothing but gigantic jaws
or a canyon where every river disappears/

But I am walking toward you
    (since you cannot be avoided).
I am singing on the way.

DOYLE POINT

I've lived in the Doyle Point Cemetery
   14 years
and never seen so much as a sheet
in the air after midnight.

I take turns sleeping in grassy places
above or between   graves not sunken
don't like them sunken.

Pines keep me company
in spring shrubs flower
for squirrels and robins
and for me.

The stones wait out the storms
but I can use the toolshed if
I want and the little stove in there
just for clipping grass
and warding off vandals   bad boys
from the village.

When I go down to the village
people look the other way
some of them are coming up
where I live one day too.

But I don't gloat.

I visit the new graves
before the flowers wilt
see them at their best and
don't embarrass residents
like I did when they were living.

It's up to me to throw the rotting flowers
down the slope
and trim around the stones
so I know them
same as you know your own street.

Wonder what they'll write
on my stone.
Some lie likely.
Doesn't matter.

I've got the place picked out though,
beside that crabapple.
It knows how to flower
how to live.

IN WOODS

Lived in woods
sang poems to
hold off the lonelies

when stars blinked out and
barred owls talked of my ending

Woods greened and made more
in forever shadow

    I blinking in meadows afraid
of innocent branches
a leaf pile
    learned the washing of brooks
    on hard feet

    introduced to the night
    when
moons came to my evenings

Spiders taught me their webs
and at last the old oaks
brought me religion

    I
probably died sometime
wrapped in fecund soil and used-up leaves

I never noticed the death
here in woods
moving closer
to towns

Towns!
you think you have won
    but
We take you back
we take you back

AND AFTER THAT

If I lie down in cold tide one thick January—
 reach of trees reflected
 tattooing my still arms—
there will be a single cloud
 seen many times in sleep.

Gulls live on the island I would pass

In an ice river near the sea
 if I lie down
there will be no alarms,
 no outcries on city streets,
 no exclamation.

The ice will glisten
  the slim trees sigh
 in their stiff coverings

After that the water will form
  oleanders from my best breaths
 and after that—
  I will not feel the chill

GHOST LEG

A twisted leg is removed
    there is blood but I do not die
       my flesh touches grass
A rose fragile full of light
    waits in my hand
I have not lost a single petal

There is air where my leg was
    my skin touches water

I prophesy a doom that
      no one can amputate from me
    though night resounds with magical stars
    though morning is fed out of
    sunscattered sky
    I can reach only as far as a rose.

I am walking on sea bottoms
    dragging this legshadowed in seaweed
      dragging this leg will not warm
wherever I go
    this leg will not warm

ICE AGES

. . . How a man died every time they spit rock
every time the long-haired dogs howled
out of cold moist nights—

how in ice ages
         ribbons of water glazed
      all mountains
the valleys set up that morose echoing
      no one recorded.

It was all foretold:
    how a man would die, then
    a woman give sweet birth
    whenever winter winds spit their rash splinterings.

Some of the caves held out where
half-mad ones crouched till spring,
    till floods
carried dog carcasses downhill to lodge
in the busted trees.

That was the name of our history:
iced winters tumbled together in
    a dirge followed by
    a deliverance and
    a freshet spun into air
helping us forget maggoty dogs,
cave-dark death,
helping us stay blind to every closed corner.

MIDNIGHT

is the heave of hallways
in the dusty dark
a lunatic telling lies
that strip April's new blossoms
before dawn

MIDNIGHT
rides a piebald horse
through canyons
their rims seething in orange smoke

MIDNIGHT
lives on the underside
of oceans
waiting for
a clock's soft stroke
time
for attack

TWISTER

Too late to run.
Knelt in irrigation ditch,
joined hands—

Cloud spiral heaved a shed door
over their haymow. . .

Three-year-old snatched from his mother's
scream, her grasping fingers—

Looked for him days
beside smashed barns,
upended trees,
houses ground to flinders. . .

Looked for him weeks,
looked for him months—

He was like the storm:
gone,
gone for good.

MARCH FLOOD

Walking tomorrow
    from breakfast to sleep
    in rain and
    in rain and
    in rain …
           The StonyKill's high …

Houses stand stunned in the water.

New people will come to
    weed gardens—
    work on drainage
    —set tea kettles to boil

Walking tomorrow
    from breakfast to sleep

But this town's deserted.
      The StonyKill's high,
        brimming over, and
houses stand stunned in the water.

EPIPHANY

It could be the tallest pines
needle-shimmering,
fasting in frozen February.

It could be the aimed heron, neck
set forth in flight;
a heron, hunting a glance from blazing water.

It could be the undoing of clothes,
long couplings, confused heat,
tangles of shudderings, of thrusts.

It could be a refinement of decorous flowers,
quiet and bursting,
or silk on the fingers,
an outpouring of chill water.

It could be any day, any hour; age-dried
    or youth-juicy—
It could be here, it could be now.

MINNEWASKA, BURNING

It rained all day.
Still, the mountain blazed,
      dimmed
  in smoke, in fog

They lost the great house,
firefighters reckless and worn
    in June rain—

long tracks of their trucks
filling with mountain mud.

Pink and white mountain laurel
were woven in woods
          almost
to the leftover chimneys of Wildmere
the day Minnewaska took fire.

June showers laid the dark dust,
the turquoise lake lay
clean to its depths, no longer
reflecting the bleached hotel, so
long abandoned.

Fireman left with their weariness
and no one in the valley could see
what each one saw clear
in the night of his skull:

Minnewaska,
     haven of hawks,
     the sweet
     and the wild;

Minnewaska, burning

FEVER TREES

He found a trail among the fever trees
    a trail in a tangle where
    an opulence of cheetahs lay.
Macaws called overhead in density
      of clotted green
    and voluptuous vines caressed
      the fever trees.
He found at last the unknown,
Unexpected he could love
    in summer's forest shimmer
    among the drugged insomniacs,
      the fever trees.

COMMUNION

It's cold
you're hungry
    chance my open palm
your toes tense your
black legs hardly
thicker than a thread

Sideview eyes beneath a crown
as black
don't leave my face and
nearly frozen hand
that doesn't tremble

You take a small peck
at a finger
judging material
beneath your weightlessness

You grasp a seed
    fly in a blurt of wings
Above me your toes clamp a twig
as you batter the seed covering

Fragments fall for your fellows
and for the summer
sunflower that will be

It's breathless when you come
trusting or daring
a foreign country

How will I know next time
it's you testing my cold hand
my hungry openness?

LOW CLOUDS

Low clouds pour toward the sun
cold mountains underneath
    SUN
scalds dim clouds with brilliance
rubbed raw after ages

Low clouds, long rumpled mountains
        and below
a town tacked down with gray churches
untidily pinned to the landscape with
    denuded trees, smudges of
    pines, hemlocks

As clouds burn away, a sky
blue as a nest of improbable dreams
remains.

That sameness—Eye of God—
is a sum of all our hours,
    all our stories

makes the oldest religions and myths
turn out to be true,
terrifying
wonderful

THE SEARCH

This is the fourth time
I have come to this place
looking for you.
     It is a house
full of rooms,
     fireplaces,
kitchens and narrow bedrooms.

I have been here before
and it is a house for
lost ones.
     There are many people.
Most of them sit in the public rooms
by windows watching the grounds
as snow fills the spaces.

We move about an enormous
secret.
I bent to gaze into
their faces. They don't mind.
Some smile, showing old teeth or
no teeth.

Sometimes a flicker of you
lies in a tight age-spotted hand.

You and I rent an apartment.
We will stay here together.
I am happy but wonder
if we can get along.
     Then I find
out you have been murdering people.
Bodies of women lie under the floor
boards and
a few legs stick up from the floor.

I am frightened. The police come.
Will they blame me?

All of the bodies are women, all
are you, slightly altered.
Of course you have left me again
to tell my incredible story.
In the dream this time I'm weeping

because you grew older,
because you could not keep yourself
free from your greatest fear.
    I have come here four times
looking for you. How could the *you*
I remember ever be gone?

CAN COLLECTOR

He wins his war again
with cans he sells.

He lost his house
    because he signed a paper,
        like before.

He has the barn,
the land around it,
and he prays.

Some days, everything is made
for him—a miracle—

but he won't sign anything.

In Dachau, praying,
    alive/dead,
    dead/alive,
        he hung on
    though the Germans made him sign,
    took all he had.

Escape was his first miracle.

In America years afterwards
he asked a dentist to pull
his 14 teeth.
            Kicked out for indigence,
he pulled the 14 teeth at home
with pliers, praying
past the blood and pain.

Cans. He first saw them in a dream.
Now, cans found in garbage
heap in a baby carriage that he liberated
from a dump.
Cans pay his taxes.

At night in his unheated barn,
prayers warm him.
Days he hunts leavings out of dumpsters,
    fears food poisoning, but
prayers make him indestructible.

He doesn't marvel. "I'm 200 million times better
than I was," he says (meaning, at making miracles).

If he lives a little longer,
he'll never have to die.

THE AMERICAN GOAT WOMAN

She was old, and she lived with goats. People called her goat woman. She lived off goat milk. She made head cheeses, and spun goat hair into yarn and wove the yarn into cloth.

In the part of the day when the sun grew flat upon the earth, she took out her goatskin pouch with its bones and smooth stones, feathers of eagles, teeth of raccoons, claws of bobcats that prowled round her cabin at night. She cast them as dice into a circle she'd outlined in dirt at the back of her house, so that the last rays of the sun winked on them red, binding them close with long shadows.

By night she'd be far into a trance, the wings of great birds cooling the fevers that all day grew thick in her head. Her way was the laying of ghosts who cried out to her on those nights when she walked over prairies to bury chicken's eyes, or to pour day-old blood onto rocks in the shine of the great molten moon.

She quieted spirits that jerked inside tombs, that moaned in the summer's sweet air, that bled on her doorsteps, that carved sleep out of the hours of night so that her eyes hung deeper and deeper in flesh that seemed burning.

She could not remember the day she had come there. She'd tended the goats all her life. In the path that led nowhere but up and down hills into prairies and at length into mountains were places she'd lain with the goats, with the great black puck that mounted her as the sun mounted mountains.

Strange demons she birthed, and strangled them all. She used up their bodies to appease the dead spirits that spoke to her while she walked dreamless, striding through little towns, the goat herd behind her.

The living stayed still behind doors till she was well gone from their walls, and the stench of her out of their nostrils. Such a one cannot die, they would say; for hadn't their grandparents told of the ancient goatwoman whose cabin they'd burned? She had come then with curses she hurled into all of their faces as she passed by. She had caused a dam to break then which flooded the valley, destroying many. All of them knew how the animals fled at her coming; how the wild goats she commanded could never be caught, and would attack any lonely wanderer who walked out on the prairie.

She was old, the goatwoman. She laid many ghosts, for her potions had power. She has passed from that country, those times, taking all the goats with her, some say into caves by the froth of the sea. In the shine of the moon, on the edges of winter, the rocks still turn rusty. The wailing of those who are dead turns into stillness and waiting.

UNDER THE BED

There was a place under the bed where the floor grew darker. He could put his foot into it, and not touch bottom. It was cold beyond cold.

Once he went in up to his hip. There was a sound like wings, and claws tore at his thigh. He pulled himself out, and he was greatly afraid.

Before he could stop her, his cat ran under the bed and disappeared. He could hear her for hours, crying somewhere under the floor.

Cursing, he tore at the floorboards, but the dark place got bigger. He decided to burn down the room and destroy the dark place.

He poured gasoline and stood at the door, trying to light a match. There was a wind in the room that blew the door closed, and the match wouldn't light.

Like sands in an hourglass, everything in the room began moving toward the dark place. He hung onto the windowsill for a long time . . .

CANOPIES

Rips in the sky make
trees bloom too soon
lava smokes into the sea

Under the great canopies
we're waiting with
our blazed eyes and seared faces

Even the poems are hot

Political candidates promise shade
without new taxes
cures for common fried skin syndrome

Fish in our nets
are already cooked
and our geese too

Venus our older sister   now
and beings who watch these nights
will see two
evening stars

DAD'S GHOST

didn't bother looking
in our refrigerator for beer
didn't light up a Camel either

He went outside to tinker with
Mom's Chevy which
of course he'd never seen
being dead before
it was built

He said he
recognized the house—
it's much the same—
stared at the new grandchildren
told me it takes
some getting used to
being younger than your daughter

People don't age
wherever he's been
since that hospital day
when his blood broke and
he drowned trying
to run from himself.

I wasn't afraid of Dad's ghost
it limped a little
as if its pale body
was a poor fit

IMAGO

After he died she saw him
running for a train

You're still alive
she shouted but
he didn't hear

He wore a tan uniform
Soldiers chased him but
the train slowed for him

and he leaped on board
rushing through
empty cars

But they got on too
followed him
to the end

where he leaned over
the railing
watching escaping tracks

They raised their
rifles and he turned
smiling

He wavered and she thought
he fell
instead a huge
imago took his place
unfolded shimmering wings
became the air

beyond the train
flying in spurts of sheen
out of the picture

After that she
never saw
him

THE BACK BEDROOM

The boy clutches his collie pup
climbs the stairs to
the back bedroom

Dreams ride here
some too dark
for the living

Can he catch death
like measles
sleeping here?

The pup squirms loose
runs down to light
the easy voices below

The boy waits on the stairs
trying not to cry
   not to remember

At a touch
light springs up
to comfort

"Here, Buster!" he calls
Will the dog come
does the dog fear him

now that he's next
to the yawning deep
of beckoning?

There is no softness
in this room
though his brother's bed
is gone   is gone
is gone
an echoing
sends the boy
rushing downstairs
into a well of warmth

"Buster wouldn't come,"
he tells the watching
adult faces

LIVED IN A TREE

I lived in a tree   a tall hemlock
I slept tickled with soft needles

in a hemlock grove anchored
above a wide fall of water

where deer slept close to a swampy retreat

I learned climbing from tree
to tree   slower than squirrels
high as nests   encountering
snakes   looking with them for eggs

No wonder after days in the
tree's crown
I thought I could fly

It was easy living in my tree
hard bark on my cheek
ants inquiring about my fingers

I sucked them from the backs
of my hands   ate morels
drank rain pools   found berries
went hungry

Deer rubbed their antlers on my hemlock
owls glided by clutching
blood in their beaks

I came to my end
reclining among branches

leaving my satisfied skeleton
wherever scavengers let fall
the bits of me

under evergreen trees

SEA SONG

I lived on the beach
as soon as I saw
the tumbled ocean   the whitened shells.

My eyes and mouth were sand
my familiars laughing gulls   sand pipers.

As wind combed and recombed the dunes
I waded far out to hunt hermits
in low tide   discover periwinkles
on kelpy rocks.

It was no bother to live on the beach
damp cold   sand and storms no trouble.

It was like swimming in my own
comfortable blood   finding myself so enlarged
so unaccountable small.

The gulls and I studied each other
I gentled the horseshoes back to water
hoping for them

wore necklaces of shark's eggs
ate mussels and clams
my house scallop shells and
bleached driftwood

every day full of salt
and surf sounds. Some nights the moon
walked on the water.

I followed my courage into the storms
till one in a gigantic froth
took me back
and after many washings
left me on another beach—

not a bad death   considering

THEY CAN NOT SEE ME

Leave them behind   walk
under forsythia   dig down
with moles and bulbs

with earthworms and small snakes
striped with their stories

So much room!
I cannot imagine daylight
forget the sun's every day ravishing

how small I become
inconsequential   even happy

I come out only with night things
to bawl for moon kisses
to examine stars

to tongue blood between my teeth

As hair grows
they can not see me
thinking me a crazed beast
a link gladly forgotten

Now even the stars are not
reference points
Earth
our only mother
points me true

I swim in moist dirt
wear it under my armpits
lie in it for my rest

Many tunnels
much air
tiny nuggets to eat

I couple with whatever comes
No more impossible dreams

It is all dreaming

I am really gone this time
They can not see me

FROM "THE MARGARET POEMS"

*The Margaret poems came about because of an overheard
conversation between two office workers at Marist College one Friday
afternoon. They were discussing what they'd do on the weekend. One said she ex-
pected to watch Margaret. I wondered if Margaret would be
interesting to watch . . .*

I

Margaret lost her lease
and decided the Stone Ridge Supermarket
was the handiest place to live.
She took a lot of Perrier into a storage room
and camped out under the potatoes
Before long the meat man's helper
told on her.

After that she hung out at the p.o.
and the bank lobby until
closing time   Then she followed an office girl
home and watched her all weekend

II

While Margaret was a restroom attendant
at The White House
Queen Elizabeth made a formal visit.

Margaret realized she bore an uncanny
resemblance to the monarch. . .
When Elizabeth Regina went to the toilet
during a state dinner
Margaret locked her in and
enjoyed a lot of mutton and hasty pudding before
the queen somewhat flushed
reappeared.

The sovereign refused to press charges
against Margaret for impersonation though
saying, "She quite reminds me
of my sister."

III
Margaret decided to become a juggler.
She performed on the sidewalk
a couple of blocks from Luchow's.

She wasn't very good at juggling
and nobody would have watched her
for long except that
she was juggling bank books.

Until the police arrived,
she had a large crowd.

XXXI--A HUMONGOUS FUNGUS

Margaret contracted a skin disease
her doctor said was fungus

It grew underneath her clothes and finally
crept upon her face

She used the salves and ointments
all the creams he recommended

The fungus would subside
then work its way in rooted network
to the surface, popping up in unexpected spots
on her chin or beside her ear

its red return
itchy and tracing itself over and over
into her dreams

What could Margaret do?

One ad promised nostrums
beyond belief   She believed them

Inside the wizard's basement office
she sat among dusty bottles and ill-smelling vials

of toad toes (she supposed) and salamander spit

The wizard was himself well-warted
and could have been a reptile in a former

form. She paid $50 for a stoppered tube
of tea leaves he told her to brew

in fullest moonlight only
Then she waited for the waxing moon

to shine upon the pustules on her face

She drank tea sips and wetting fingertips
with its bitterness
applied a smear to every reddened bit of skin

Two days she dosed and stayed away from mirrors.
Meanwhile she felt a facial glow that made her wonder

At last she ventured
to look upon her own reflection

finding there small and flourishing
mushrooms which soon fell away

She gathered all of them and
found that taken with a vegetable sautée they taste
wonderful   To grow them needs the dark

and then the tea and then
the moon just right

Her lifestyle is somewhat
transformed but she

thinks of herself
as garden more than woman

"It is a different world view"
she tells whatever friends she may invite

to sample her mysterious fungi. They munch happily
but have learned from her past adventures
not to ask questions.

XXXXIV--CICADAS

Margaret wanted to discover the secret 17-year lives of
cicadas, underground years
when they were
supposed asleep, waiting
for resurrection

Though no one really knew how the subway singers
        spent their
6,000 darkened days

Margaret did not fear.
She picked a few brown bodies out of their
songs as they
hummed on fence posts or cottonwood trees

They squirmed but
Margaret spoke kindly to them
promising
them dignity in her research

Electronically she recorded every speech her cicadas made
no matter what hour of day or night
Tapes sang back
and the cicadas wildly signalled
their own recorded voices

Margaret dreamed these conversations until
she began making the same sounds herself
and couldn't stop.

Taking her as one of their own
cicadas sat on her shoulders teaching her everything they
thought or
remembered
including
their lives during the long wait
for world entry

As a result Margaret became
the foremost expert in cicadas,
the only recognized recorder of
the insects' under earth years

She wrote *17 Years with Earth's First Spelunkers*
revealing that the earth is hollow
made so from investigations by aeons
of cicadas digging
through dirt,
dislodging enough rock to
create volcanic action at Mt. St. Helen's
movement of tectonic plates and
earthquake in Los Angeles

She also wrote persuasively
the cicada's personal saga
     extraterrestrial and wise

It was, she wrote, cicadas who watched time
unravel from its original
yarn ball, chased
according to them
(as interpreted by Margaret)
by The Great Cat in the Sky
Goddess of All

Margaret barely avoided
becoming guru to the rich and famous
and could hardly scrape off followers
of what they swore was enlightenment
a new religion

But she did escape, no one quite understands
how   Some say she was carried off by
cicadas into Earth's
great hollowness where
she could be looking for
China

or maybe not

YEAR 96

Words drizzle across the page
forgetting themselves halfway
home. She has been alone too long.

Someone in the family comes
to stay, has a job
with changeable hours,

is often gone.

She doesn't know when
he'll be back.
Finds him
gone when she gets up,
gone when she
goes to bed--

she could be
dreaming him--

   takes vitamins
to restore
connective webs
broken through,
catching nothing

Last entry in her
diary: (Aug. 14, 1981)
"Foggy day."

FRIENDS

I'd walk her home.
She'd walk me back.
Next time, we'd stop halfway
to sit on a culvert
by the old town hall.

Dark by now,
the village quieted around us.

What did we talk about
all those hours?
Fireflies wafted over the field
behind the Andrews' house.
Honeysuckle hung in the air
and a few dogs barked.

We didn't have wheels
or steady boyfriends.
I wanted college for myself,
she didn't. Her family could have
sent her. Mine couldn't.

She and I had maybe a year to go
before big changes came.
We couldn't wait

REFINEMENTS

Entitled to refinements at my age I
lurk around the numbers games
wondering what signs to read
for greater wealth

One morning turkeys gather
at roadside several of them
small   watched over by
the larger who scramble through
field fences first

One day the hummingbirds
don't show up even the old long-necked one
although I sit half of an afternoon in wait
remembering she tried to chase me off
once   That brave minute
in all the slitted openings that time allows

It isn't always birds of course
Yesterday missing pets came back
along a darkened highway smiling
full of burrs and happy exhaustion
ready to let me pick off sticktights and
grumble at their waywardness

In classics class today a student said
in answer to my question on the bafflements in *Genesis*
"Ask God" and there revealed
a whole philosophy: Don't sweat the big stuff

"In the last days
all signs fail," I read
and sure enough the numbers don't add up
to any fortune and I'm left with ordinary slipshod signs
that Whitman says are notes from The Divine
conundrums with few and yet persistent clues

So I am refining my position
deciding that for now frail courage has to do
what feeble faith cannot
and build a better fortune from
the bricks at hand

BEFORE I WROTE

Before I wrote
my hand bled
scraping rock for words

Books I'd read lay in pools
     fading to pulp

Now that I write
my skin wears
where pens rub

Words build in all directions
I explore mazes

Books with my name
age fast   and
if my hand bleeds
I can use blood

ABOUT THE POET

Shirley Powell began her lifelong poet's journey in third grade in an Ohio hamlet called Reilly, and her first poems appeared in newspapers and in a collection of school children's poems published by the state's department of education. As an undergraduate at Miami University in Oxford, Ohio, she won two prizes for poems written in college. From then on, she was hooked on poetry. A major part of her writing life emerged when she moved to New York City in 1971. She became an active Greenwich Village poet as the surrealistic and subterranean found their way alongside her lyrics. Narrative poems flowed from these as well, and around age 40, she began to publish poems in magazines. Since then, she has been involved with poetry workshops, public readings, a literary quarterly *(Oxalis),* and with managing various poetry reading series, festivals and contests in her Upstate New York years. Four books of poetry preceded this volume.

www.ingramcontent.com/pod-product-compliance
Lightning Source LLC
LaVergne TN
LVHW041200080426
835511LV00006B/680